What We Have in Common

A Brim Coloring Book
Written by Jane Landey
Edited by David Austin
Drawings by David Austin and Jane Austin

Copyright©2017

Published by CreateSpace: An Amazon Company.
Printed in U.S.A.

Introduction

What We Have in Common. Br.im Coloring Books enable children to color the drawings as they read along! The books display the similarities of related animals. In this series, the hedgehog and the anteater are compared. The facts enable children to appreciate common values. Thus, imbibing in them interest towards animals which could help them to appreciate what they have in common with one another.

THE HEDGEHOG

AND

THE ANTEATER

The hedgehog and the anteater are small animals. They have spikes on their bodies. They fold up when enemies come by.

The hedgehog and the anteater meet early one morning on a rich soil in Africa.

I am a hedgehog.

I am Echidna, the Anteater.

I live in the bush.

I live in the bush too!

I could roll myself and hide.

I could hide myself too!

My body has spikes.

My body has spikes just like you!

I can smell with my nose.

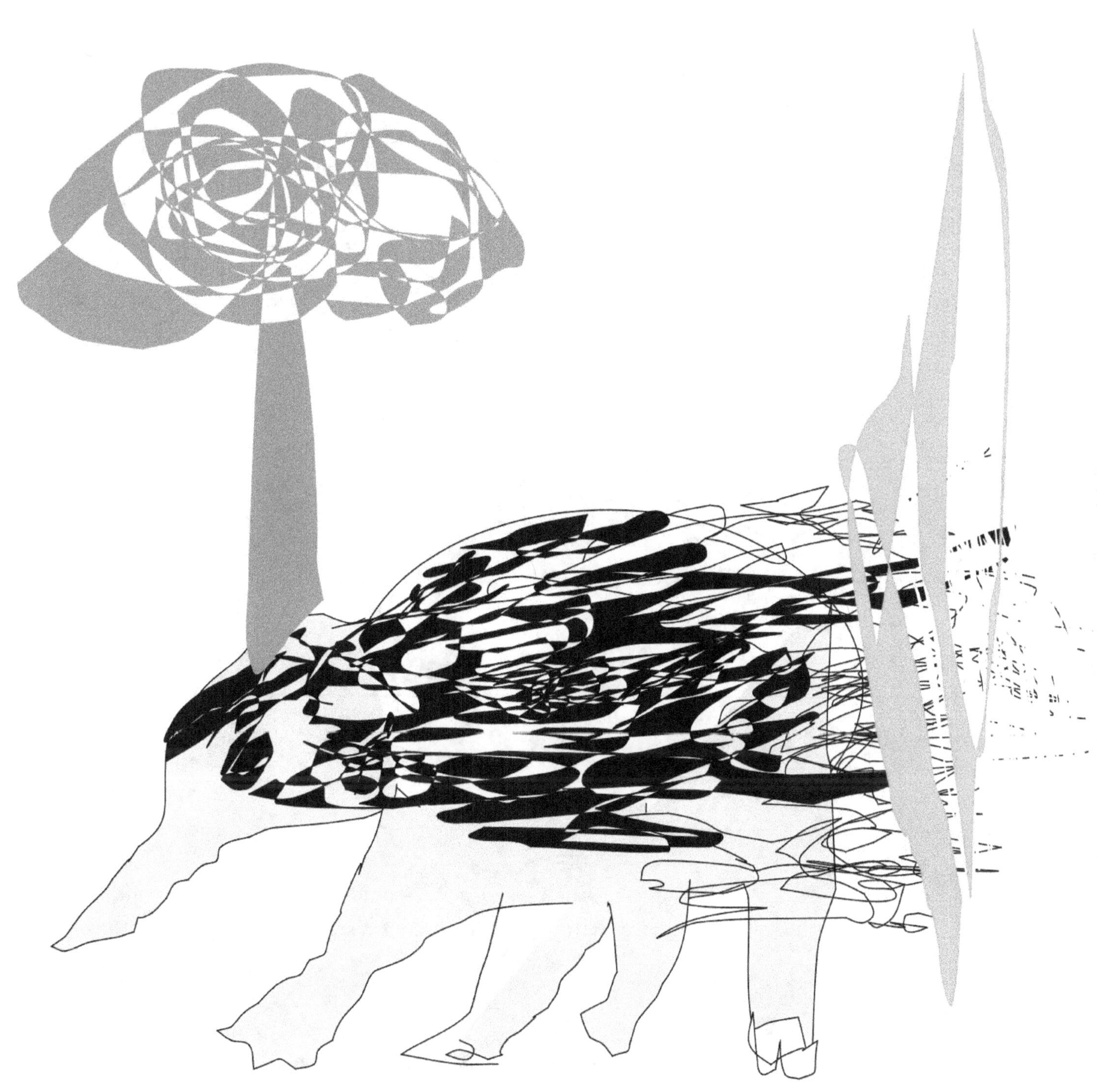

I can smell with my nose too!

I eat ants Mister
Anteater.

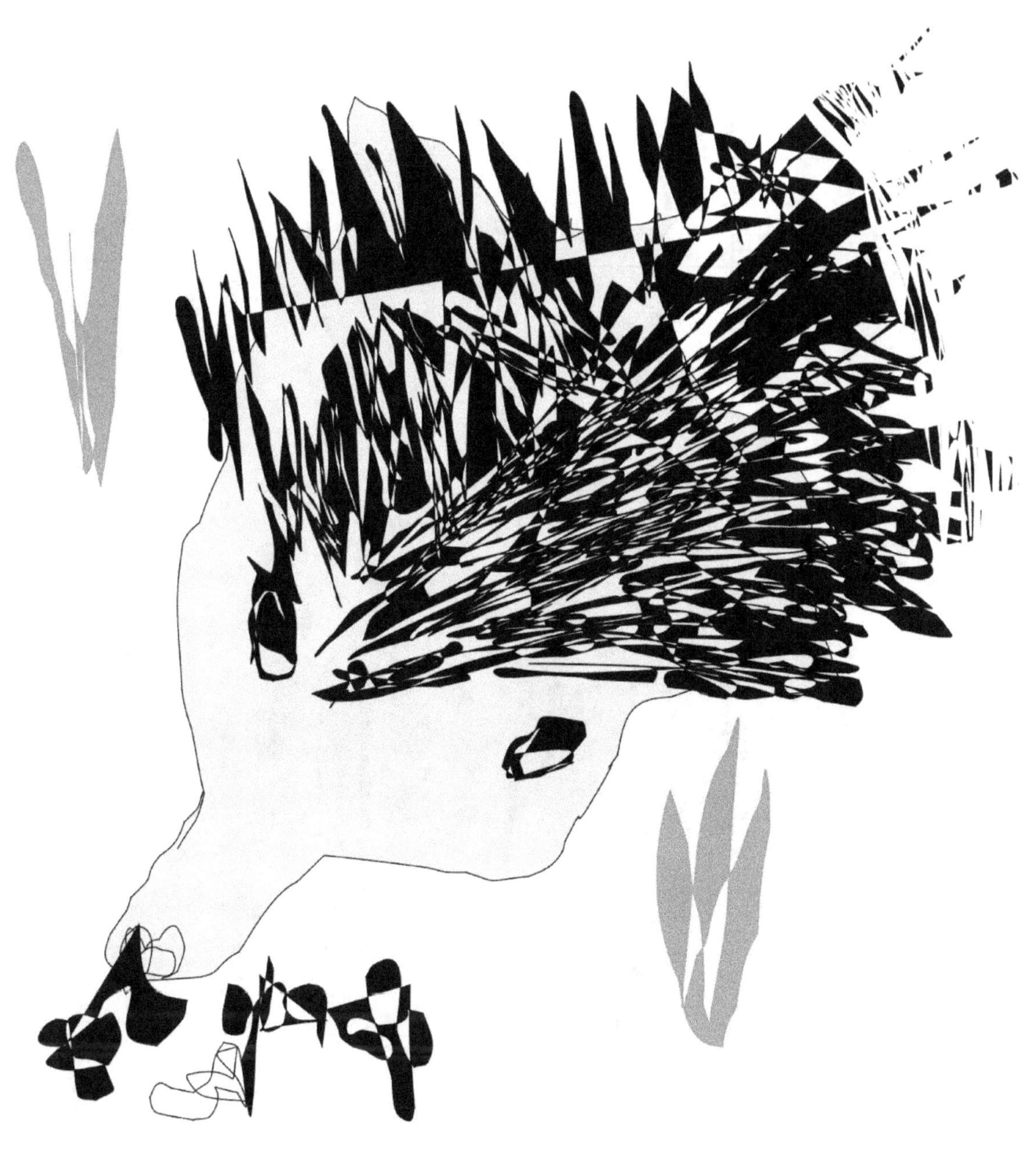

So do I Mister Hedgehog!

Is that why people call you
Echidna the anteater?

Yes, because I eat lots of ants!

No one can see me.

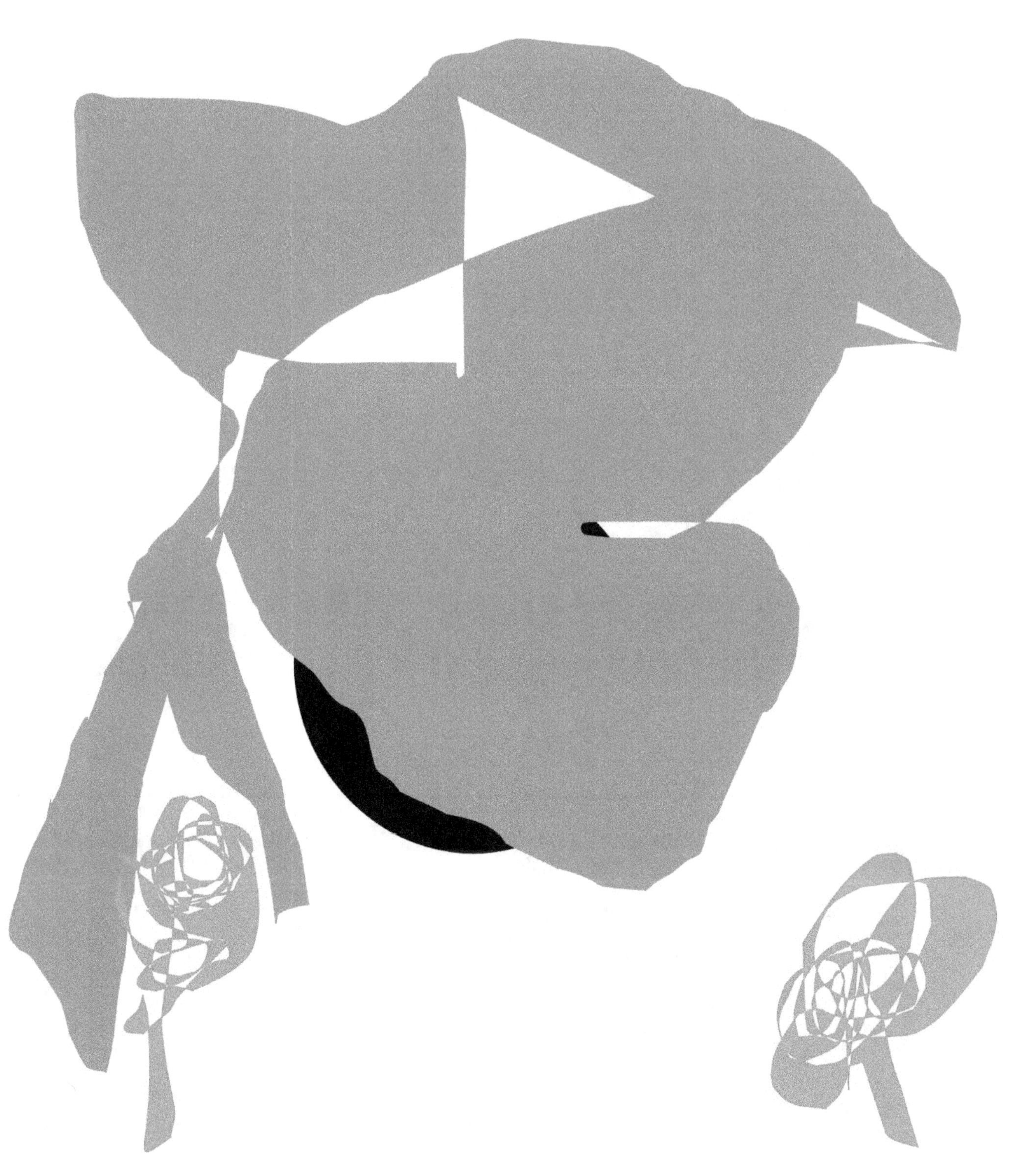

No one can see me either!

Look at me!

You look at me too!

Let's run!

Alright!

One, two, three!

Go!

My legs are too small!

My legs are too fat!

I must rest!

I am waiting for you!

I want to sleep Mister Anteater.

I want to look for more ants!

Okay, I love to do the same!

Here are some, Come over!

Hummmm, delicious!!

What We Have in Common Brim Coloring Books

Crocodile and Alligator
Turtle and Tortoise
Starfish and Octopus
Worm and Snake
Turkey and Vulture
Ostrich and Emu
Weka and Kiwi
Bat and Rat
Camel and Llama
Duck and Pelican
Kangaroo and Wallaby
Pig and Tapir
Skunk and Squirrel
Hedge and Anteater
Cat and Owl
Elephant and Rhinoceros
Dog and Fox
Buffalo and Bull
Leopard and Cheetah
Horse and Zebra